Grade **3.1**

Scott Foresman

Decodable Practice Readers 1-15
Volume 1

Scott Foresman
is an imprint of

Glenview, Illinois • Boston, Massachusetts • Chandler, Arizona
• Upper Saddle River, New Jersey

ISBN-13: 978-0-328-49220-6
ISBN-10:   0-328-49220-5
8 9 10 V011 14 13 12
CC1

Contents

UNIT 3

A Winter Picnic

Written by Beth Banlin

Short Vowels Syllable Pattern VC/CV

Molly	Hansen	dinner	winter
cannot	suggest	picnic	basket
happen	plastic	splendid	mittens
button	traffic	napkin	supper

High-Frequency Words

the	said	would
to	a	are
you	warm	here
friends		

1

Molly Wade liked Rose Hansen. Rose always
waved as Molly waited for the bus.

"Jane," said Molly, "I would like to ask Rose
for dinner."

"It is so cold," Jane said. "Rose will not go out
on a cold winter night.

"It is hard for Rose to get around when it is
slick. She has to use a cane."

Molly finds Mom at the stove. Corn is in a
pot, and hot ham is in a pan. Mom cuts a carrot
and puts it on a plate. Mom has made plum pie.
Yum!

"Are you sad, Molly?" Mom asks.

"No, Mom, but Rose might be sad. She is alone and cannot come here for dinner."

"We can go to Rose," Mom and Jane suggest. "We can fill a picnic basket and take it to Rose. We can eat with her. We can make a picnic happen."

Molly gets the big picnic basket. Jane puts in plastic plates, forks, and cups. Mom fills it with ham, corn, and carrots. Molly adds napkins.

"We can surprise Rose. A winter picnic in a warm home will be splendid."

"Molly, take a blanket. Jane, take the basket," Mom said. "I will hold the plum pie."

Molly, Jane, and Mom get hats and mittens.

"Button up, kids! It is cold. There is no traffic, but it is slick. Take care as you cross."

Molly raps on the door.

Rose Hansen smiles. "Come in!
You all must be cold. Are you wet?"
Molly smiles. "We have food.
Can we eat by the fire?"

Rose tells Molly, Mom, and Jane to sit by the fire. "It will make you warm."

It is time for dinner. Molly takes out plastic plates. Jane takes a napkin, cup, and fork.

"Good food and friends!" Rose smiles.

"It is not just supper," said Molly. "It is a winter picnic!"

Summer Picnic

Short Vowels; Syllables VC/CV

sudden	summer	picnic	Calvin	tablet
basket	plastic	napkins	fabric	velvet
bedbugs	Jensen	public	traffic	splendid
after	catnap	sunny	windy	foggy
happens	cannot	sitting		

High-Frequency Words

a	she	said	of	to
you	again	are	there	from
they	was	your	could	have

Mom had a sudden idea. "It is a swell summer day," she said. "It is a picnic day!"

Dad said, "Yes! Calvin, grab that pen and tablet. We will make a list of stuff to take."

"Our picnic basket will be on that list," Calvin stated. "And plastic cups."

"Napkins go on our list," said Mom.

"We will need fabric to sit on," added Dad.

"Is velvet fabric?" said Calvin. "We can use my old velvet Mighty Hero cape."

9

"Yes, velvet is a fabric," said Mom. "But you might use that hero cape again. We can take an old bed quilt."

"Are there bedbugs on it?" joked Dad.

Mom got the picnic basket and napkins. Calvin grabbed plastic cups and the rest of the things on the list. Dad grabbed that old quilt.

Mom drove to Jensen Public Tree Grove. There was not much traffic. Dad set the picnic quilt next to a big tree. Calvin got the basket from the van.

After they ate, Calvin rested and said, "I think I will catnap in the sun."

Just then, it was not sunny. It got windy and foggy! "I hate when that happens!" said Calvin.

Calvin felt big wet drops! "I cannot catnap in this mist," said Calvin, sitting up.

"Grab the basket and quilt — fast!" yelled Mom. "This picnic is over!"

"Too bad you did not take your Mighty Hero velvet cape, Calvin," said Dad.

"Why?" asked Calvin.

"You could have slipped it on. Then Mighty Hero might have stopped the fog and saved the day," said Dad.

Mom and Dad smiled. Even with wet fog, Mom, Dad, and Calvin had splendid fun.

Melvin Is Splendid

Short Vowels; Syllables VC/CV

Melvin	helmet	dentist	splendid
Marvin	trumpet	lesson	comment
Nutmeg	tennis	mascot	rabbit
winner	velvet	sudden	hubcap
zigzagged	Lentil	public	cannot
basket	upset	hectic	

High-Frequency Words

put	a	to	do	was
work	have	one	you	the
of	your	said		

Melvin put on his helmet and got on his bike. He had a lot to do. His first stop was his dentist.

"Those teeth look splendid, Melvin," smiled Doc Marvin. "Keep up the good work!"

Melvin ran back to his bike, put on his helmet, and rode to his trumpet lesson.

"I have just one comment," Miss Nutmeg told Melvin after he played his trumpet. "Splendid! I will see you at the show at six."

Melvin smiled! Melvin ran back to his bike and put on his helmet. His next stop was the tennis game. Melvin's club had a match. Melvin was the club mascot. He got dressed as a big rabbit. In the end, Melvin's club came out the winner!

"Splendid!" yelled Melvin.

Melvin jumped back on his bike. He put on his helmet. It was close to show time. Melvin was riding home to get his velvet vest. He had shopped for it just for this trumpet show.

All of a sudden, Melvin ran over an old hubcap. His bike zigzagged. Crash!

At six, Miss Nutmeg was at Lentil Hall looking for Melvin. Lentil Hall was the place for the trumpet show. Miss Nutmeg spotted Melvin. He was jogging next to his bike, and he was filthy!

"Your public is ready," said Miss Nutmeg.

"But I'm a mess," protested Melvin. "And I need my velvet vest."

"You cannot get that vest," said Miss Nutmeg. "You must get on stage and play that trumpet!"

Melvin grabbed his trumpet from his bike basket. He began to play. He felt upset that he did not have his velvet vest, but he just played.

"Splendid," yelled Melvin's fans. "Splendid!"

It was a splendid day! Hectic, but splendid!

Frogs, Flies, and Foxes

Written by Sean Kenton

Decodable Practice Reader

2A

Plurals *-s, -es, -ies*

lunches	farms	miles
plants	grasses	bushes
animals	ladybugs	inches
rabbits	babies	bunnies
foxes	flies	boxes
dishes	grapes	

High-Frequency Words

are	the	to	there
you	many	of	have
do	a	one	two
they	oh		

"Lunches are in the basket. The basket is in the car. Hop in! It is time to go," Mom tells Jan and Sam.

On the ride, Jan rests. Mom and Sam see things as Mom drives. Mom and Sam see farms and miles and miles of corn.

Sam asks, "Will we get there by ten?"

Mom nods yes as Jan wakes up. "Are we there yet? Is it time for lunch?"

"Not yet," Mom tells Jan. "But you will like the State Park. It has many plants. It has grasses and bushes. It has lakes. Lots of animals have homes in the park."

Sam and Jan run. Mom yells, "Stop! Do not go yet. I need to get the basket. Then we will hike together."

"Will we see animals, Mom?" Jan asks.

"Yes, we will see tiny bugs and big animals too."

"Ladybugs! Ladybugs!" Jan holds a ladybug.
"Mom, it is red like the buds on the bushes."
   Bugs jump in the grass just inches from Sam.
"They sure can jump high!"

Rabbits hop in the grass. Jan and Sam see babies. One, two, . . . five baby bunnies hop.

"Is that a dog, Mom?" asks Jan.

"No, Jan, it is a fox. Lots of foxes live here. "Most often we do not see foxes. They nap in the day and hunt at night."

At the lake, frogs eat flies. Lines of ants take bits of food to their hills. It is time for lunch at the lake.

At the lake, Mom, Sam, and Jan sit on the blanket. Sam and Jan take the boxes and bags Mom has for them. Dishes hold grapes. Yum.

Tiny fish swim in the lake. Jan and Sam wade in. Jan bends to get a fish. Oh! Oh! Jan sits in the lake. Sam and Mom get her up. Jan is wet, but the hot sun gets her dry.

Boxes and bags are in the basket. It is time to go. Mom holds the basket. Sam and Jan hold hands as they go to the car. Mom, Sam, and Jan had the best lunch ever.

Jon and Jill

Plurals –s, -es, -ies

things	lists	dots	bunnies
Buses	nests	plants	dogs
cats	pennies	bikes	mommies
dresses	kids	glasses	baskets
boxes	trees	tablets	babies

High-Frequency Words

they	what	to	do	of
a	you	want	put	the
one	know	have	are	their
your	said	two		

Mom spots Jon and Jill. They just sit. "Summer is not fun. What is there to do?" sad Jon asks Jill.

"I cannot think of fun things," sad Jill tells Jon.

Mom makes a list on a tablet for Jon. Mom makes a list on a tablet for Jill.

"Take these lists," Mom tells them. "Go hike. As you spot things printed on these lists, put dots next to them. Can you find these?"

Jill jumps up and yells, "I will find them, Mom."

21

Jon just grins.

Jill and Jon hike. Jon spots plastic bunnies.

"Did Mom want live bunnies or fake?" Jon asks.

"Mom just printed *bunnies*," Jill tells Jon.

The kids put dots next to *bunnies* on the tablets. Then Jon and Jill pass Tell Public School. Buses sit by Tell School. Jill and Jon put dots next to *buses* printed on the lists. "I saw those buses first!" yells Jon.

Jon and Jill spot nests, red plants, dogs, cats, old pennies, bikes, mommies in dresses, big kids in glasses, bike baskets, milk boxes, and elm trees.

Jon and Jill put dot after dot on those tablets. In a bit, just one thing is left. It is *cute twin babies*.

Jill and Jon did not spot cute twin babies at first. But they know that the Jensens have cute twin babies. The Jensen home is by Tell School.

Jon and Jill race to that home. Dad Jensen is on an old quilt on the grass. So are the cute twin babies! Jon and Jill put dots on their tablets.

"Hi, kids! Your mom said you might stop by. She gave me notes for you," Dad Jensen tells Jon and Jill.

Those notes said, "Is summer fun now?"

"Yes!" yell Jon and Jill.

Dad Jensen smiles. He tells his cute twin babies. "One summer, I will make lists for you two, too."

Hal's Glasses

Plurals –s, -es, -ies

glasses	bugs	plants	spots	ants
hands	legs	boxes	baskets	stones
axes	bags	bats	mitts	trees
grasses	kids	caps	stoplights	dresses
mommies	babies	robins	flies	dimes
pennies	buddies			

High-Frequency Words

does	to	have
what	were	the
do	are	

Hal does not think this will be fun. He has to slip on his new glasses. He did not have glasses before this.

Hal slides his glasses on. Yikes! His glasses stun him! What Hal sees stuns him! Hal can see stuff he did not see before!

Hal asks Dad and Mom if he can walk home. Hal hopes he can see stuff. Mom drives the van home so Hal and Dad can walk.

As Dad and Hal walk, Hal is happy! Hal spots bugs on plants. Hal did not see bugs before he had glasses. Now Hal can even see bugs have red spots!

Hal sees ants. Before he had glasses, ants were just black spots to Hal. Now he holds an ant in his hands. Ants have legs!

As Hal and Dad walk on, Hal spots tan boxes and baskets by an old white van. Hal slips his glasses off. The tan baskets and boxes now look like tan stones.

Next Hal sees five men with axes and bags. Hal slips his glasses back on fast. Five men do not hold axes and bags but bats and mitts!

Hal likes his glasses. He sees trees, grasses, kids, red caps, stoplights, nice dresses, mommies and babies, robins, flies, and even lost dimes and pennies.

As Dad and Hal get close to home, Hal spots Mom. Mom stands by the van and waves at Dad and Hal. Next to Mom stand Hal's buddies. His buddies wave at him too. Hal waves back. His glasses are so swell!

Teaching Bell to Behave

Written by Neil Fairbairn

Our puppy, Bell, hopped and jumped like a big rabbit! It was the strangest sight. But as Bell got bigger, friends did not like her jumping on them. Bell needed to start behaving.

We taught Bell to sit. This was not the hardest lesson for Bell. Dogs will sit if you hand them dog bones for sitting. We would hold a dog bone high up. "Sit!" Every time Bell sat, we gave our puppy a dog bone. "Good dog!" We did this lots of times. Bell was getting lots of bones.

Then we gave Bell harder lessons. Bell must stop and not go when told "Stay." We started off with sitting lessons. We made Bell sit and gave her a bone. Then we put a hand up and cried, "Stay!" We stepped away. If Bell stayed, she got dog bones. If Bell did not stay, we tapped her nose. "No, Bell, no!"

We were trying to make Bell come. "Come."
We tried and tried to make Bell come. If Bell
came, we gave her bones and made the biggest
fuss. Soon Bell was sitting or coming at our
command. Bell was getting lots of bones.

It was time to test Bell. Would Bell sit, stay, and come when we were not at home? We found out at Ben Lane Park. We let Bell run and run.

We yelled, "Come, Bell." Yes, did you see? Bell came right up to us. Bell is a smart puppy!

The last test was the hardest. We told Bell to sit and stay. We tried hiding. Bell tried to find us again and again. At last Bell just sat as she was told. She stayed. Bell got lots of bones!

It takes time for puppies to learn. But we are glad we gave Bell lessons. Bell used to hop on laps of friends. She used to jump on them. We no longer see her hopping on laps or jumping on friends. She runs up and sits. We are happy, and Bell is happier!

Miss Kline

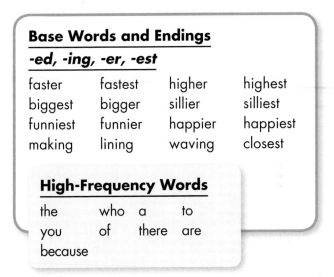

Base Words and Endings

-ed, -ing, -er, -est

faster	fastest	higher	highest
biggest	bigger	sillier	silliest
funniest	funnier	happier	happiest
making	lining	waving	closest

High-Frequency Words

the	who	a	to
you	of	there	are
because			

It is class picnic time. Miss Kline tells the class, "We will have fun! We will find who runs fast, faster, and fastest!"

Miss Kline has kids lining up by her. She holds a red flag.

"When I yell 'go,' run to my red flag," instructs Miss Kline.

Kids get set. Miss Kline yells, "Go!"

Kids run fast. Miss Kline runs fast. She runs to an old tree waving the red flag.

Ann runs past the flag. Then Max and Leo run past. Miss Kline yells, "Ann ran fastest!"

Ann smiles and tells Miss Kline, "No, you did! You ran past us with the flag."

"Oh," Miss Kline grins. "I did not think of that."

Next Miss Kline jumps high and sets the red flag up in an old tree.

"We will jump at my red flag," Miss Kline grins. "Who can jump high, higher, and highest?"

Kids jump one at a time. Scott jumps closest to the red flag. "Scott jumps highest!" Miss Kline yells.

Scott smiles and tells Miss Kline, "No, you did! You set the red flag up there."

"Oh," Miss Kline grins. "I did not think of that."

That happens all day. Miss Kline thinks Patty skips the biggest steps, but Miss Kline skips bigger. Miss Kline thinks Bill tells the silliest joke, but her joke is sillier. Miss Kline thinks Val can do the funniest trick, but her trick is funnier.

As the picnic ends, Miss Kline tells the class she is happy. But Ann tells her, "We are happier because you are fun, Miss Kline."

"Oh," Miss Kline grins. "That is making me even happier."

"That makes you happiest!" yells Miss Kline's class.

Big Men

Base Words and Endings

-ed, -ing, -er, -est

stopped	opened	looking	grabbed
bigger	heavier	biggest	dropped
spotted	sliding	asked	printing
looked	melting	slipped	coming
freezing			

High-Frequency Words

a	one	the	from
have	been	why	are
would	said	were	

On a hot summer night, an old red van drove up High Hill by Bess's home and stopped. Three men got out. One man opened up the van. When he did, mist started coming out from it. And Bess saw that the van held odd boxes.

Bess kept looking as a big man grabbed an odd box from the van. It looked heavy. The big man did not drop it.

Then a bigger man grabbed an odd box. For an instant, Bess felt like he might drop it. It might be even heavier than the first box. But the big man did not drop his box. He kept it in his big hands.

Next the biggest man grabbed an odd box. Bess felt it might be the heaviest box. It just might have been! The biggest man dropped it! Bess smiled. The biggest man dropped his box! Bess spotted it sliding fast down High Hill!

But Bess asked, "Why are boxes so heavy for big men? And why would a box slide so fast?"

Bess read printing on the van's side. It said, "Fred's Frozen Food."

Bess looked at the men's hands. The men had mittens on.

Now it made sense! The boxes might not be so heavy. The boxes were freezing. Yet frozen boxes must be melting on this hot night. That is why an odd box slipped from the big man's hands, and why frozen food in an odd box went sliding down High Hill!

Goat Art

Written by Angela Lowen

Vowel Digraphs *ee, ea, ai, ay, oa, ow*

grown	goat	mean	own	train
keep	roam	free	beep	road
stay	meal	rows	bean	seeds
feasted	grain	loads	hay	feed
way	pain	coat	afraid	bleated
paint	tree	green	feet	display
week	eat	peas	oats	pays

High-Frequency Words

was	a	does	to
oh	the	of	what
do	you	one	friend

Billy was just a kid when Ann got him. Now
he is a grown goat. He is a big, bad grown goat.
Billy does not mean to be bad. He just likes to get
his own way. Ann tried to train Billy and keep
him safe. It was a big job.

Billy did not like his pen. So Ann let him roam. Ann let him run free. Ann heard "Beep! Beep! Beep!"

"Oh, no! Billy is on the road." Ann rushed out and grabbed Billy. Ann tried to make him stay in the yard.

Billy made a meal of everything. He ate the plants in window boxes. He dug up and dined on rows of bean seeds. He feasted on grain Mom tossed to the hens. He fed on loads of hay in the barn. Mom called him "Billy the Pig."

What did Dad say about Billy? "Billy gets my goat."

"What do you mean?" Ann asked.

"I mean Billy upsets me. Billy makes me mad. Billy eats the feed. Billy gets in my way. Billy is a pain. He gets my goat!"

Ann petted Billy and patted his coat. "Billy, I am afraid that Mom and Dad will sell you. You need to be good."

Billy bleated.

One day, Ann went out to paint with Billy.
Ann tied him to a tree. Ann took out her paints.
Billy got in them. He bit the rope and got yellow,
green, and red feet. He stepped on her picture.
"No, Billy, no!"

At home, a friend saw the painting. "I like it. It
is different. May I take it? I will pay for it."

He gave Ann $5. Yes, Billy can paint!

Now Ann lets Billy get in the paints. Billy paints with his feet every day. Ann sells his Goat Art. Ann takes it to art fairs. Ann sets up a display. Ann made $150 at a fair last week.

Now Mom likes Billy. "He can eat the peas, beans, and oats."

Dad likes Billy. "He is a fine goat. He pays his way."

Billy and Ann make a great pair!

Gail's Birthday Treat

Vowel Digraphs: *ee, ea; ai, ay; oa, ow*

Gail	sleeping	dreaming	real	yellow
Sleepy	pillow	streamed	window	know
day	birthday	yippee	cleaned	braids
green	jeans	gray	sneakers	bowl
peaches	cream	toast	eating	coat
road	train	meet	treat	seats
Main	Street	exclaimed	squeeze	
roast	bow	own		

High-Frequency Words

was	a	you	what
to	said	your	do

Gail was sleeping a bit late. And she was dreaming. Gail dreamt she had a real yellow puppy.

"Gail!" called Mom. "Wake up, Sleepy!"

Gail sat up on her pillow. Sun streamed in her window.

"You know what day it is, right?" asked Mom.

Gail jumped to her feet. "Yes, it's my birthday! Yippee!"

"Let's get this day going!" said Mom.

Gail cleaned her face, fixed her braids, and then dressed in green jeans and gray sneakers.

In the kitchen, Mom gave Gail a bowl filled with peaches and cream! Then Gail had toast.

When Gail finished eating, Mom said, "Grab your coat. We will hike up the road to the train. We'll meet Granny in the city."

"Granny!" called Gail. That was a birthday treat.

Gail and Mom found seats on the train. They rode to Main Street by Granny's.

"Happy birthday, Gail!" exclaimed Granny. Granny gave Gail a squeeze. Then Granny gave Gail a birthday gift. It was a stuffed yellow dog. It was almost like the dog in Gail's dream, except it was not real.

"Thanks, Granny!" Gail said.

Later, Granny, Mom, and Gail went home to meet Dad for dinner. Dad was making pot roast. He showed Gail a basket. "I do not think it came in the mail," said Dad.

Gail peeked in the basket. Inside was a yellow dog, a real yellow dog. It had a bow around its neck! "Your own yellow puppy, Gail," smiled Dad.

Granny and Mom grinned. Gail's dream was real!

Ray's Trip East

Vowel Digraphs: *ee, ea; ai, ay; oa, ow*

Ray	wait	stay	Gleason	East	Coast
three	stream	blow	float	leave	thirteen
week	slowly	painted	railings	mowed	each
day	unload	nails	street	leaf	scream
knee	pain	Gray	afraid	really	sprain
explained	feet	complained	easy	say	road
meet	see	sleep	dream	leaned	pillow
glow	streaming	window	greetings	beamed	loaf
flown	laid	least			

High-Frequency Words

could	were	there	lived	to
the	was	said	you	have
you'll	from	here		

Ray could not wait! Mom and Dad were sending him to stay with his pal Gleason on the East Coast. Ray was going to stay there for three weeks! Gleason lived by a big stream. They were going to blow up rafts and float in the stream.

Ray planned to leave for Gleason's in thirteen days. The first week passed so slowly! But Ray helped with chores while waiting for his trip. He and Dad

47

painted fences and porch railings. Ray mowed the grass. Each day, his trip felt closer!

On the day before Ray was to go to Gleason's, he helped Dad unload bags of nails from the truck. On the street, Ray slipped on a damp leaf! He fell and let out a small scream!

Dad ran over. "My knee is in pain," said Ray.

Dad picked up Ray and drove him to see Doc Gray. Doc looked at Ray's leg.

"I'm afraid it's a really bad sprain, Ray," explained Doc Gray. "You must stay off your feet for weeks."

"But I'm taking a trip to the East Coast," complained Ray.

"This isn't easy to say, Ray," stated Doc Gray. "But you will have to stay home."

When Ray and Dad got back home, Mom ran out to the road to meet them. "You'll see Gleason next summer," she said.

"Thanks," said Ray. He went in to sleep.

The next day, Ray woke from a dream. Ray sat up and leaned on his pillow. Gleason stood in the glow of sun streaming in the window!

"Greetings, Ray," beamed Gleason. "I'm here to loaf around with you and your sprained knee!"

Mom and Dad came in. "We had Gleason flown out," Dad explained. "You may be laid up, but at least you will have a pal around!"

Clint's Clam Chowder

Written by Chelly Bergstrom

Vowel Diphthongs /ou/ou, ow, and /oi/oi, oy

Joy	hour	chowder	choice	found
how	pound	mound	amounts	flour
boiled	mouth	now	counters	scoured
loud	noise	outside	shouted	bounce
bounded	voice	down	sound	wow
town	brown	frown	house	proud
boy				

High-Frequency Words

a	wanted	to	have
what	said	would	of
there	was		

49

Clint had a nice plan to make supper for his mom and dad. He wanted them to be glad. Clint asked his sister Joy to help him. Joy was glad to help Clint make this fine meal for Mom and Dad.

"We have an hour to make supper. What will we make for Mom and Dad?" Joy asked.

"Mom likes clam chowder best," Clint said.

"That would be Dad's choice too," Joy added. "How can we make chowder?"

"We will use our heads," Clint said.

Clint found the page that told them how to make the best clam chowder. Joy chopped a pound of clams. Clint added a mound of fresh things. They put in just the right amounts of cream, flour, and spices.

Joy set the big pot on the stove. When the pot of chowder boiled, the smell made Clint's mouth water.

"How long now?" Clint asked.

"We must not rush," Joy pointed out. "Good chowder takes time!"

Clint cleaned counters and scoured dishes. He set out bowls and spoons for the chowder. Then there was a loud noise outside.

"It is Mom and Dad!" Clint shouted. With a bounce in his step, Clint bounded to the front door to greet them.

"What is that wonderful smell?" Dad asked in a happy voice.

"Joy helped me make clam chowder!" Clint yelled, jumping up and down with glee.

"I like the sound of that," Mom added, setting down her shopping bags and hugging Clint.

"Wow, this is the best meal in town," Dad said when Joy gave him his big brown bowl.
"Chow down while it is hot!"

There was not a frown in the house. Mom, Dad, Joy, and Clint ate every last drop of that clam chowder. Clint was a proud boy that day!

Roy, Dad, and Scout

Vowel Dipthongs /ou/ spelled *ou, ow;* /oi/ spelled *oi, oy*

Roy	outside	ground	flower	brown
found	town	snow	snowy	snowplow
down	tower	proud	join	around
frown	count	enjoy	spouted	house
plow	Scout	boy	voice	shouted
power	loud	noise	growled	choice
south	pointed	sounds	downtown	bounced
oil	counter	how		

High-Frequency Words

the	was	been	today
whole	a	would	have
to	of	you	into
you're	said	are	your
here			

Roy woke up and looked outside. The ground was white! Yesterday the ground in Mom's flower garden had been brown. Today, Roy found that his whole town was under deep snow.

On snowy days, Dad had an important job. He drove a snowplow! When Roy spotted snow outside, he knew Dad would have a big day.

57

Roy ran down to the kitchen. Dad was getting set for his day. Big, strong Dad stood like a tower over Roy. Roy was proud of his dad.

"Can I join you today, Dad?" asked Roy.

Dad turned around and gave Roy a silly frown. "Can I count on you to enjoy the day?"

"Yes, sir!" spouted Roy with a smile.

Roy and Dad left the house and went out to the snowplow. It was big! Dad named his plow "Scout." Dad helped Roy up into his seat. When Dad got inside the plow, he looked at Roy.

"You're my first mate, Roy, my boy," said Dad in a stern voice. "Are you set to plow?"

"All set," shouted Roy. "Power up the plow!"

Dad turned Scout on. It let out a loud noise. The big snowplow growled with power!

"We have a choice," said Dad. "We can plow north or south. It's your choice, Roy."

Roy pointed south. "Sounds good," said Dad. "Downtown is that way. Here we go!"

Dad dropped Scout's plow down to the ground. As Scout plowed the street, the whole truck bounced a bit.

Roy and Dad plowed all morning. "We will stop for gas and a bit of oil," said Dad. "And then we'll sit at that counter in that diner for lunch. How about that?"

Roy enjoyed snow days! He liked to help Dad plow the ground!

Joyce Paints

Vowel Diphthongs /ou/ spelled _ou_, _ow_; /oi/ spelled _oi_, _oy_

Joyce	found	town	oil
moist	soil	choice	cow
counted	clouds	sound	oink
loud	crowding	around	louder
brown	ground	mound	flowers
sprouted	background	down	plow
coiled	frowned	spoil	However
flowerpot	mouse	wow	voice
shouted	proud	enjoy	pointed

High-Frequency Words

a	from	the	of
was	one	were	to
into	you	who	

Joyce found a new hobby. Painting! Her family had a farm far from town. Joyce took her oil paints outside. She laid a blanket over the moist soil and sat. She had a choice of things to paint. The sky over the cow field was one. Joyce counted six big, fluffy clouds over it.

Just then a sound came from the pigpen. "Oink! Oink!" Those pigs were always loud! When they were crowding around their food, they were even louder. Joyce had never painted pigs. Now pigs were her choice!

Joyce started by painting brown ground. Then Joyce added a fence that went around the pen. Mom had planted a garden on a mound next to the pigpen. Flowers sprouted from that mound. Joyce painted the mound and flowers.

In the painting's background, Joyce added Dad's old broken-down plow. At last, she painted pink pigs and their coiled tails.

Joyce had just finished when her hand slipped. A big, ugly brown paint drip found its way into a lower corner on her painting. Joyce frowned. Did she just spoil her painting?

However, Joyce had a plan. She painted over that brown spot and it became an upside down flowerpot. On top of that flowerpot, Joyce painted a mouse. The painting was not spoiled!

"Wow!" a voice shouted. Joyce turned to see her big sister, Bettie. "That painting is good, Joyce! I'm so proud of you!"

"Thanks," shrugged Joyce. "I enjoy painting."

Bettie pointed at that mouse in Joyce's painting. "I like this critter best," smiled Joyce.

Now it was Joyce who felt proud!

"Me too!" said Joyce.

Jason's Music

Written by Sharon Tell

Syllable Patterns V/CV, VC/V

Jason	music	tiny
even	pupils	talent
finish	silent	never
focus	rapid	family

High-Frequency Words

to	a	the	could
give	of	some	was
would	again	you	said
were			

Jason had always liked music and hoped to play it well. Even as a tiny boy, Jason liked to sing and play. He pounded the keys. He even made up his own tunes. Mom and Dad asked for less noise. Jill shouted, "Stop!" But Jason did not stop. He played and played.

Then Mom and Dad said yes. Jason could try music lessons. Jason borrowed a trumpet. Mr. Reese could give him lessons. Mr. Reese had lots of happy pupils. Jason started classes. Jason tried some notes. But horn music was not the music for him.

Jason tried to play music on a flute. His flute made odd sounds. Mrs. Lee told him, "You have so much talent. You will play well." But Jason did not finish his lessons. Flute music was not for him. He needed to play music, but not on the flute.

Jason stopped playing music. He seemed sad. Jason had not found the best music for him. The house fell silent. Mom and Dad longed for more noise. They longed for a louder house. Mom and Dad worried that Jason would never make music again.

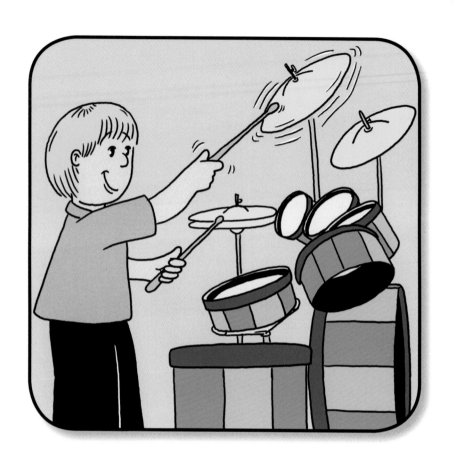

Ms. Bates suggested a new way to make music. Jason went to class. Ms. Bates showed him a drum set. Jason smiled. Jason tapped small drums. He hit big drums and pounded even bigger drums. Jason and his drums made loud music!

Ms. Bates seemed pleased. "You need to focus on drum lessons," she said. "You are a good pupil. You will play drums well in no time."

Jason had lessons each week. He played rapid and slow beats on his drums. He started playing music with the class band.

Loud noises from his drums filled the house day and night. But his family did not care. Mom and Dad tapped their feet. Jill hummed. Mom, Dad, and Jill were quite proud of Jason. Jason was making music again!

Megan's Robot

Syllables V/CV, VC/V

Megan	table	report	major
Texas	river	meters	study
music	lazy	grader	robot
pupil	clever	paper	super
human	silent	baby	rival
magic	seven		

High-Frequency Words

the	was	work	to
do	a	from	said
they	would	there	are
whole			

Megan sat at the kitchen table and looked at the time. It was six o'clock. Then Megan looked at the work she had to do for class. First, she had to finish writing a report. Her topic was a major Texas river. Then for math, Megan had to change a list of numbers from feet to meters. And she even had to study a new song for music.

Megan felt lazy. This was too much for a third grader! "I wish I had a robot to help me be a better pupil!" Megan said to herself.

Then Megan began to think about what that robot might do. It might read things in a rapid way and tell her what they meant. It might write her river report. It would write clever things on her paper. Mr. Lemon would think that Megan was a super writer.

And the robot might do math for Megan. It might add or subtract. It would tell her things like how many feet there are in a meter!

Her robot would play music and help her study her new song. Robot music had to be better than human music.

Megan's robot might do more than help her study. It might dust her room and make her bed. It might be a silent lawn mower or a sitter for Megan's baby sister. And it might teach her to beat rival soccer players.

Megan felt good about her robot idea. A robot would be like magic and make hard things in her life go away.

Then Megan looked at the clock. It was almost seven! Seven! Megan had wasted a whole hour daydreaming about a robot! "A robot did not help me," she said to herself. "It hurt me!"

70

A Texas Crater

Syllables V/CV, VC/V

Texas	craters	metal	iron
travel	rapid	magic	planet
tiny	damage	climate	human
major	second	United	secret
level	meters	study	visit

High-Frequency Words

a	you	what	the
some	are	from	of
they	have	to	was
there			

In Texas, you can find craters! What is a crater? It is a large hollow spot in the ground. Some craters are made when an object from space hits land. That object is a meteor.

Meteors are big chunks of rock or a metal like iron. Meteors travel at a rapid speed in space. Meteors may go so fast that they burn up. You may have seen meteors burning in the night sky. These meteors are called shooting stars. Shooting stars might seem like a space magic show!

71

If a meteor does not burn up and crashes on a planet instead, its name is changed a little. It's called a meteorite. Most meteorites are tiny specks and will not cause much damage. But some can be much bigger. A large meteorite can cause real problems and even change our climate. That might affect human life.

A major crater is close to Odessa, Texas. It is the second largest crater in the United States.

For a long, long time, the cause of this big hole by Odessa was a bit of a secret. It was not until around 1920 that people realized this big hole was an old crater. A meteorite crashed there thousands and thousands of years ago.

When that meteor hit, it dug a hole about 30 meters deep. That's more than 100 feet below ground level! This meteor left a hole that is about 170 meters wide. That's almost as long as six football fields!

Humans study craters to find bits of meteorites. Those bits of rock and metal tell us interesting things about outer space.

You can visit museums that display bits of meteorite. When you do, remember that a meteorite came a long way to visit us.

From Farm to Table

Written by Karen Schwartz

Syllable Pattern Consonant + *-le*

apples	table	simple
little	ladle	sample
bottles	handle	kettle
middle		

High-Frequency Words

to	the	have
of	answer	one
a	buy	are
people	they	some
two		

Is going to the store fun? Supermarkets have rows and rows of jars, bags, and cans. We can get baked rolls, apples, beans, meat, and more at supermarkets.

It takes lots of steps for food to get to our table. These steps start at the farm.

Take an apple. It can be red, yellow, or green. It grows on trees. How did it get from tree to store? The answer is simple.

Start at an apple farm. Apples grow on apple trees. Little apples get bigger and bigger. Big apples get ripe.

It is time to pick ripe apples. At one farm, we can pick apples right off trees. We can fill a basket and pay for the basket of apples.

At the farm stand while we pay, a big bowl is filled with apple cider. We use the ladle to fill cups. Sip. If we like the sample, we can buy bottles of cider.

At most farms, workers are paid to pick apples. These apples are sent to big sorting houses. The apples are cleaned, sorted, and loaded in boxes. The boxes are loaded on trucks and sent to stores. People at the stores handle the apples with care as they place them on a table. Grapes and lemons are on tables as well.

Some apples are made into other things.
A big kettle might be filled with apples. Apples
are cooked and made into jelly. Apples are
baked into the middle of some pies and cakes.
Cut apples are dried and sold in bags.

We can get dried apples and apple pies and cakes. We can get apple jellies and apple drinks. We can get just plain apples. We can find them at the store.

Take an apple or two or more. Pay for them. Now we can take apples home.

Mom cleans and cuts apples. We dip and eat the apples. Yum. We are glad that apples made the trip from farm to table.

Nell, Chuck, and a Puzzle

Final Syllable –le

Noble	little	bugle	single
apple	Maple	chuckle	juggle
middle	fumbled	puzzle	possible
handle	riddle		

High-Frequency Words

a	to	have	said
was	the	of	other
they	what	into	

After lunch, Nell came up to Mr. Noble. "I have a little problem. My bugle will not play. I am not able to blow a single note," she told him.

"Not a note?" asked Mr. Noble. "I'll have to check that bugle."

Mr. Noble started to get up to look at Nell's bugle when Chuck ran up to his desk. "Mr. Noble," Chuck said. "A mouse stole my apple."

"A mouse in Maple School?" asked Mr. Noble with a chuckle. "Tell me how."

"Well, I had my apple," said Chuck. "And I was using it to juggle. But in the middle of a juggle, I fumbled it."

"And then?" asked Mr. Noble.

"Well, it just flew away!" said Chuck. "And I think a mouse took it."

Nell was still waiting for help with her bugle. "Mr. Nell, my bugle is more important than an apple!"

Mr. Noble smiled and looked at both kids. "I think this is an interesting puzzle," he said.

"My bugle?" asked Nell.

"My apple?" asked Chuck.

Then Nell and Chuck looked at each other. "That is not possible," they both said.

In the hall, Nell picked up her bugle by the handle. Then Mr. Noble, Chuck, and Nell looked in the end of the bugle. They saw a red apple.

"That is why my bugle will not play a single note," said Nell.

"And that is what happened to my apple," said Chuck.

"But how did the apple get into the end of the bugle?" asked Mr. Noble.

That was a real riddle!

Cattle Creek Museum

Final Syllable –le

Cattle	little	buckles	eagle
beetles	circles	fiddles	sample
gentle	saddles	saddlebags	bundle
bridle	handle	bottle	bubbling
chuckle			

High-Frequency Words

you	said	to	the	was
of	are	a	into	here
some	what	were	been	

"Let me show you our cowboy stuff," said old Mr. Toby to Dad and the kids.

Mr. Toby was in charge of Cattle Creek Museum.

"Are you a cowboy?" asked little Dana.

"No, just an old cowboy fan," explained Mr. Toby as he led Dad and the kids into the museum.

"Here are our cowboy belt buckles," said Mr. Toby. "Look closely and you will see belt buckles with eagle designs on them, or beetles, or fancy circles."

"Cowboys wore fancy buckles?" asked Denny.

"At times in town," explained Mr. Toby. "But not out on the cattle trail."

"Are those fiddles?' asked Dana.

"Yes, some cowboys played fiddles and sang," said Mr. Toby. "I will play a sample cowboy song."

Mr. Toby gave a button a gentle nudge and the sample played for a bit.

Then Denny looked at cowboy saddles and saddlebags. "Those bags can hold a bundle of cowboy stuff," said Mr. Toby.

And Dana was studying a bridle. "What are bridles?' she asked.

"Bridles were leather straps that cowboys put on horses' heads. A bridle helped a cowboy handle his horse," said Mr. Toby.

Dad spotted an old dented tin canteen. "Look, kids. This holds water for a cowboy," he explained.

"Like a bottle?" asked Dana.

"Yes, cowboys filled canteens in bubbling streams of clean water," said Mr. Toby.

"I would like to have been a cowboy, but I'm afraid of horses!" exclaimed Denny.

"Me too!" said Mr. Toby with a chuckle.

The Scarecrow

Written by Sheldon Cline

Compound Words

scarecrow	roadway	outside
sunshine	rainstorms	peapods
campgrounds	weekend	farmhouse
roadside	someone	anybody
haircut		

High-Frequency Words

a	of	the
were	their	to
you	oh	someone
anybody	who	was
there	have	they

85

Scarecrow rested on a pole in rows of pea plants near the roadway. He hung outside in sunshine and rainstorms. He waved crows away from the peapods.

Ron and Dad were on their way to Calvin Campgrounds for the weekend. Ron pointed at the scarecrow as Dad drove by. "See it, Dad?" Ron asked. "Can you see it?"

Just as Dad and Ron passed the farm, the car started to tremble and bump down the road.

"Oh, no," moaned Dad. "We need to stop. Maybe we can get help at that farmhouse. Stay near the car, Ron."

As Dad made his way to the house, Ron spied wild berries by the roadside. He got out to take some.

Then Ron heard someone speak, but he did not see anybody. "Who is it? What did you say?"

"Do you need help?" the scarecrow asked as he tapped Ron.

Ron jumped. "But . . . but," Ron mumbled.

The scarecrow was dressed in rags. He had a
pumpkin head, and he had on a cowboy hat. He
had long hair made of hay. He needed a haircut!
"Let's see if we can fix the car," he said.

Ron and the scarecrow went to the car. The
scarecrow looked at it. He found an oil can.
"A little oil here and a little oil there. It is fixed.
Now it is time for me to go home." He stumbled
to his pole and winked at Ron.

Dad came out of the farmhouse. "We have to wait for help," he told Ron.

"Try it, Dad. I think it will start and run right." Dad started the car and it purred.

"That is funny," Dad noted. "The car is fixed! How did you know, Ron?"

Ron just smiled. It was his secret.

Dad and Ron drove off. They will be at camp by sunset. Ron smiled at the scarecrow.

Ron waved goodbye, and so did the scarecrow!

Recess?

Compound Words

oatmeal	rowboat	playground
anything	baseball	backstop
outfield	homemade	centerfield
daydream	shortstop	strikeouts
grasshopper	understand	backyard
understood	basketball	

High-Frequency Words

the	other	anything	do
there	where	to	one
again			

Ms. Surges told her class, "At afternoon recess, we will study compounds like *oatmeal* or *rowboat*.

The kids looked at each other. Study compounds at recess! That did not seem right.

But on the playground, Ms. Surges did not say anything about compounds. She had the kids play baseball. She stood by the backstop and told

Stella, Josh, and Isabel to play outfield. She had other kids get out the homemade bases.

"Can I play centerfield?" asked Josh.

"Yes," replied Ms. Surges. "But do not daydream out there, Josh."

Then she told Ronnie to play shortstop and told other kids where to play. "I will pitch," Ms. Surges explained.

Ms. Surges threw easy pitches. She did not try for strikeouts. When Tessa hit a ball hard on the ground, Ms. Surges yelled, "That looks like a grasshopper jumping from spot to spot."

On one tricky play, Kevin did not understand where to throw the baseball. Ms. Surges helped him. "My mom showed me how to play baseball in our backyard," she explained.

After recess, Ms. Surges asked, "So how did you kids like studying compounds at recess?"

The kids looked puzzled. Then Ms. Surges said, "Write these compounds in your notebooks: *playground, baseball, backstop, outfield, homemade, centerfield, daydream, shortstop, strikeout, grasshopper, understand, backyard.*"

As the kids wrote, they understood what Ms. Surges did. Tessa asked, "Ms. Surges, can we play basketball at next recess and study compounds again?"

Rainy Weekend

Compound Words

afternoon	weekend	headlights
backseat	heartbreaking	cannot
lighthouse	raindrops	thunderstorm
inside	anything	outside
sweatshirts	postcards	sunset
sunrise	seashore	sailboats
rowboats	seafood	shipwrecks
sunlight	rainbow	weatherman

High-Frequency Words

was	the	been	of	to
into	they	a	anything	here's
one	what's	are	from	said

It was late Saturday afternoon. And so far the weekend trip had been rainy! Mom, Dad, and the kids could see things out of the car windows, but not well. It was so dark and rainy that Dad had to drive with headlights on. Melinda sat in the backseat and frowned. "This weather is heartbreaking," she sighed.

Dad agreed. "We cannot even see that lighthouse in the rain and mist."

Kath looked out the window as Dad parked by the lighthouse. "At least I can see the light flashing on top."

The family ran between raindrops into the lighthouse museum. Just as they entered, a new thunderstorm started!

Inside, the family found out a lot about the lighthouse, but they didn't see anything outside.

In the lighthouse gift shop, the kids looked at sweatshirts and then postcards. "Here's one that shows this lighthouse at sunset," said Kath. "And here's one that shows it at sunrise."

"Sun?" asked Melinda. "What's that?"

The kids saw postcards that showed the seashore, sailboats, old red and green rowboats, seafood shops on docks, and old shipwrecks.

"These postcards are picture perfect," said Melinda. "I wish our trip was."

As the family sadly drove back to the hotel, the rain slowed down. Then sunlight peeked out from behind the clouds. Best of all, Melinda and Kath saw a rainbow.

Later in the hotel, a TV weatherman said, "Sunday's sunny weather will be picture perfect."

Melinda and Kath yelled, "Yes!"

Jake's Thrill

Written by Ted Brill

Consonant Blends

street	Ford	cards	sports	store
squealed	throw	must	plans	drive
square	dream	swung	split	strike
squinted	fly	park	greeted	plate
throat	struggle	sent	squiggle	best
spray	squeak	stopping	splendid	smiled
hand	squeeze	thrill	grinned	

High-Frequency Words

you	the	into	to
there	a	would	what
was	one	two	of
said	answered	could	believe

"Did you hear?" Kate ran down the street and into the house. "Jake, did you hear? Anton Ford is in town! He is going to sign cards at the sports store on Sunday."

"You must be kidding," Jake squealed. "Anton is the best. He can throw. He hits home runs. I must see him. I am his biggest fan!"

Jake made plans. "I will ask Mom to drive us to the square. There will be a line. I will take my cards. I will take my book about the team as well. I bet Anton will sign it. I will wait and wait. I will wait the whole day. Yes! I would even be willing to wait three days. Seeing Anton is a dream."

Dreaming is just what Jake did. Anton was at bat. He swung. Strike one. Anton tipped the next pitch, but his bat split in two. Strike two. Then Anton hit it hard! Jake squinted to see it fly out of the park. Anton hit a home run. His team greeted him at home plate.

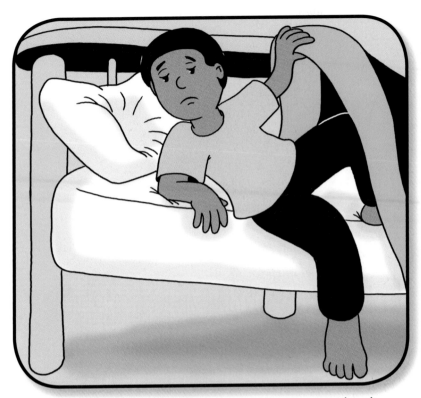

Jake woke up. His throat was sore. He had to struggle to get out of bed. Mom said he was hot and sent him back to bed.

"No, Mom, I cannot stay in bed. Anton Ford is here. I need to see him. He can squiggle his name on my cards."

"Kate can go, Jake. You must stay in bed."

Jake moaned, "But, Mom, it is Anton. He is the best!"

"No buts. Get in bed now, Jake." Mom said. "Use this spray. It will feel good."

"Hello!" Mom answered.

"Hello, is Jake in?"

"Please wait. I will get him," Mom said. "Jake, it is for you."

Jake picked up. "Yes, this is Jake."

"Jake, this is Anton Ford." Jake could not believe his ears. "I met Kate and found out that you are ill," Anton said.

Jake could just squeak. "Mom, Anton Ford is stopping by to see me. Is that okay?"

"Yes, it is splendid, Jake."

Jake smiled at Anton. Anton gave Jake's hand a squeeze.

"It is a thrill to meet you, Anton." Jake grinned from ear to ear.

"No, Jake, the thrill is mine. Meeting my biggest fan makes me happy."

Gramps's Party

Consonant Blends _squ, spl, thr, str_

throwing	Thrush	Street
squad	strong	splendid
square	spread	three
threw	SPLASH	streams
sprayed	squealed	spray
thrilled		

High-Frequency Words

the	was	a	they	been
of	whole	two	to	one
said	into	were		

Gramps just turned 75 years old, and the family was throwing a big party for him. They held it at Thrush Street Swim Club. Gramps had enjoyed swimming all his life. He had been on his school's swimming squad as a boy. Now swimming still kept him fit and strong.

In the middle of his party, Gramps's kids and grandkids sang "Happy Birthday." Then they looked on as Gramps went up to the top of the high-dive tower. Gramps was a splendid diver.

His grandkids knew which dive Gramps planned on, but the adults didn't. His whole family sat by the deep end to see Gramps's dive.

Gramps stood on a little square platform on top of the tower. He spread his arms out. One of the adults said, "I bet he does a half twist!"

Gramps's grandkids yelled, "One! Two! Three! Go!"

Gramps threw himself off that high-dive tower, but he did not dive headfirst. He went feet first. As he dropped down to the pool, he yanked his knees up to his chest and wrapped his arms around them. He made himself into a big round ball rocketing into deep water below.

Gramps hit the pool water. SPLASH! Huge water streams sprayed all over his kids and grandkids!

His grandkids squealed with delight. They knew they were going to get wet! The adults yelled with delight, too. The spray felt good on this hot summer day.

As Gramps got out of the pool, his family clapped and shouted. Gramps was thrilled! He really didn't feel 75.

Jen's Sunglasses

Consonant Blends *squ, spl, thr, str*

three	stressed	string
threw	strip	strange
split	squares	squad
streaming	thrilled	thrifty
stranger	splendid	squeezed

High-Frequency Words

could	a	said	the
should	have	of	to
anything	into	again	from
they	what	where	are
your	put		

Jen could not find her new sunglasses. Mom and Dad had just bought them for her.

Jen got her three pals in a circle. "I am stressed!" she said. "I dropped my sunglasses in this baseball field. The string that held them on must have broken when I threw the ball. I should have used a leather strip instead of string."

"Jen," Allie started to say.

Jen kept talking. "Help me find them!"

Allie did not say anything now but gave Mack and Ben a strange look and grin.

Jen went on. "Let's split this field into squares. We will each take a square to look for my sunglasses. We will be a sunglasses-finding squad."

"Jen," Allie began again.

But sentences kept streaming from Jen's mouth. "If we don't find them, I will stick lost-and-found signs up. I will explain to Mom and Dad. They will not be thrilled, but I will be thrifty and save cash to get new sunglasses."

"Jen!" Allie yelled.

Jen looked at Allie. "What? Did you see a stranger take my sunglasses?"

"No," explained Allie. "But I know where they are."

"Splendid!" squealed Jen. "Where?"

"They are sitting on top of your head," explained Allie.

Jen put her hand on her head . . . and her sunglasses. She squeezed Allie and said, "Thanks!"

Champs!

Written by G.B. Kim

Consonant Digraphs

Shasta	Beth	Cher	each
together	when	weather	Michigan
champs	she	finish	that
athlete	coach	much	machine
pitcher	rushes	trophy	

High-Frequency Words

the	are	a
one	to	who
have	do	been
of	said	

Shasta, Beth, Cher, and I run each day. We joined the track team together. We train after school. We run even when the weather is wet and cold. We are training for the big race and we hope to be this year's Michigan state champs!

We run on the relay team. In a relay race, runners wait at different places around the track. As one runner races up, she hands a stick to the next runner, who takes off as fast as she can. The last runner sprints for the finish line.

Beth is the fastest I have seen. She can take off in a flash—like a rabbit! Beth just came to our class this year, but she fit in well on our team. I am glad she is here. So is the rest of our team! Beth's speed will help our team do well in that race.

Shasta is the best athlete on this team.
She was a state running champ last year, but
she has never been on a relay team. She is afraid
of dropping the stick as she runs. Our coach
told Shasta not to think about it too much. She is
going to be fine as she races!

Cher is the best at sprinting. She will be our last runner. She looks like a machine when she is running. She goes high speed and nonstop! Cher plays a lot of sports when she is not running. She is a pitcher and a swimmer too.

I just run because I like it! I think about flying when I am running. It is nice when gentle wind rushes by my ears. Our coach said that helps me run well. When we enjoy our training, we can do our best.

This is the day of our big race! Our team has trained for weeks. Our coach thinks that we will win that trophy if we do our best and help each other. That is our goal. We cannot wait!

Behind That Wall

Consonant Digraphs
/sh/, /th/, /f/, /ch/, /ng/

spring	Beth	Mitch	North	bringing
shirt	shop	reached	crunching	chomping
thing	munching	angry	chuckled	shook
crashing	banging	smashing	shakes	those
elephant	with	mouth	gopher	teeth
thick	shark	chains	leash	beach
such	photo	them	phone	trash
catch	screeched	chicken	both	

High-Frequency Words

one	they	were	to	could
what	a	the	should	of
there	from			

One spring day, Beth, Mitch, and Granny hiked up North Street. They were bringing boxes to Gramps's shirt shop. They passed an odd tall wall that reached up 12 feet. As they passed, Mitch could hear loud crunching and chomping behind that wall.

"What thing makes such munching sounds?" asked Mitch.

"A big angry animal eating?" asked Beth.

117

Granny chuckled a bit, but Mitch and Beth did not hear her. They did hear more chomping and crunching behind the wall. The ground shook with crashing, banging, and smashing.

"What animal shakes streets and makes those sounds?" asked Mitch. "An elephant with a mouth loaded with nasty metal gopher teeth?"

"Or a thick six-legged monster shark that broke its chains and leash and stomped off the beach?" asked Beth.

Granny chuckled more. Her grandkids were such fun. She should snap a photo of them with her cell phone camera.

Then Granny and the kids saw a man rolling a trash can to behind the wall.

"That monster eats trash!" yelled Mitch.

There were more crunching and chomping sounds. "Don't let that monster catch a whiff of our tasty shirt boxes!" screeched Mitch.

Just then a loud horn sounded and a garbage truck rolled out from behind the wall.

"That truck just escaped from that steel-chomping, trash-crushing monster chicken!" exclaimed Granny.

Both Mitch and Beth grinned. Granny was funny too!

A Biography

Consonant Digraphs
/sh/, /th/, /f/,/ch/, /ng/

biography	show	that	singer	teacher	king
shortstop	with	much	she	things	birth
childhood	truth	these	this	thinking	which
matches	those	chose	path	south	change
both	photographs	photos	such	songs	finishes
fresh	choice				

High-Frequency Words

do	you	what	a	the	of
who	to	lived	was	there	were
are					

Do you know what a biography is? It is a book, film, or TV show that tells the life story of a well-known person. That person can be a president, singer, teacher, king, star shortstop, or Texas hero!

Even if a biography is made for TV or film, it still starts with a writer who studies much of a person's life. For example, say that a writer is studying Davy Crockett. She must find out things about Crockett's birth, childhood, teen years, and adult life. She must

119

find out why Crockett did things that he did. She must find the truth.

To find out these things, this writer spends much time reading and thinking about Davy Crockett. She studies times and places in which he lived. She matches those things to his life.

An important part of Crockett's life was at the Alamo. Crockett battled and died there for Texas. The writer must find out why Crockett chose to fight. What path led him south to Texas?

The writer must also find out why this battle took place at the Alamo. What change did both sides in the fight hope for?

No matter if a biography is a book, TV show, or film, it helps if it has pictures that show the person. Davy Crockett lived before there were photographs. So a writer of his story might show old paintings of him and photos of the Alamo and other such places in his life.

Writing a biography about Davy Crockett might be hard because there are many books about him. There are also films, TV shows, and even songs! The writer must hope that when she finishes her study she has fresh things to say.

If you had a choice, would you write a biography or have one written about you?

Let's Play Ball

Written by Leslie Knowles

Contractions

couldn't	hadn't	let's
we're	I've	wasn't
he'd	I'll	you'll
can't	I'm	he'll
what's	won't	you're
didn't	it's	

High-Frequency Words

pulled	a	the	some
into	was	said	to
where	very	gone	sure
you	doors	would	laughed

121

Phillip pulled on his white pants and his red top. He just couldn't wait for today's game. Last night, Phillip hadn't made a single strike. He'd felt pleased when fans in the stands had yelled and clapped. This time Phillip might even hit some home runs!

Phillip's brother came into Phillip's room. "Let's play!" Joe shouted. Joe was just three.

"We're not playing, Joe," Phillip said. "I've got a game in an hour."

Phillip tugged on his long socks. He stopped to look at himself. Wasn't something missing? Phillip scratched his head. His cap! Phillip looked on his bedside stand. His cap wasn't there. He looked on his bed. He looked under it. Where was his cap? Phillip was worried.

Mom was peeling carrots in the kitchen.
She smiled at Phillip. But she hadn't seen his cap.
Mom asked where he'd seen it last.

Phillip pictured his game last night. It was very
late. His dad had driven him home. Phillip had
gone to bed as soon as he got home. Hadn't he
placed his cap on his bedside stand?

"Look in Joe's room," Mom suggested. "I'll look in the car." No cap!

"If you'll look under chairs, I'll look under tables," Mom said. No cap!

"Coach Pepper has a strict rule: team members can't play without caps," Phillip said. "But if I'm late, he'll begin without me." Phillip's day just wasn't going as he'd planned.

Phillip's big sister Patty came in. "What's everybody looking for?" Patty asked.

"My cap. But I'm sure you won't find it," Phillip said.

"I bet I will!" Patty frowned. Then she opened doors under the kitchen sink.

"You're not helping!" Phillip said. "Why would my cap be under the kitchen sink?"

126

Patty pulled out Joe's lunchbox. It had robots on it. "Silly Joe often stores stuff here," Patty said. She opened Joe's lunchbox. There lay Phillip's cap. It looked crushed, but Phillip didn't mind. Hurray! He'd hit those home runs yet!

Just then Joe came in. "It's time to play!" he yelled.

Phillip just laughed. Now he'd know where to locate missing sunglasses and brushes—under the kitchen sink!

Let's Play This Game

Contractions

let's	I'm	I'll	you'll	it's
he's	you're	wasn't	didn't	that's
you've	I'd	won't	couldn't	

High-Frequency Words

a	said	of	woman
you'll	who	are	wasn't
was	you've	you're	who
couldn't	one		

"Let's play a game, Dad," said Trent.

"I'm up for a game," Dad replied.

"I'll think of a man or woman," explained Trent. "And you'll ask me things to try and get who I'm thinking of."

"Are you thinking of a man?" asked Dad.

"Yes. It's a man," replied Trent.

"Is this man living?" asked Dad.

"No. He's not living," replied Trent.

"Did this man play games? Was he on a team?" asked Dad.

"You're asking too much at a time," said Trent. "But no. He wasn't an athlete."

"Was this man a president?" asked Dad.

"Nope," replied Trent.

"Did this man act?" asked Dad.

"No," replied Trent. "He didn't act."

"Did this man invent things?" asked Dad.

"Yes!" Trent said. "That's right."

"Did he invent the light?" asked Dad.

"No," smiled Trent. "But he's known for electricity."

"You've given me a hint," said Dad. "Did this man also write?"

"Yes," replied Trent.

"Did this man like to fly kites?" asked Dad.

"I'd say yes," replied Trent. "I think you're getting close!"

"Did his kite get hit by a bolt of lightning?" asked Dad.

"I won't say," smiled Trent. "It's time for you to tell me who you think it is!"

"Couldn't I ask one more thing?" asked Dad.

Trent nodded. "Did he help found this land?"

"That's right," replied Trent.

"It's Ben Franklin!" shouted Dad.

"Yes," smiled Trent. "You've got it!"

Don't Be Sad!

Contractions

I'm	It's	I'll	I've	doesn't
she's	how's	you're	what's	isn't
I'd	you'd	wouldn't	let's	

High-Frequency Words

to	do	been
doesn't	you	you're
the	you'd	wouldn't
would	you're	once

"I'm home!" shouts Millie.

"Hi, Millie!" Mom smiles. "It's almost time to eat. Will you get Jess and then help me fix lunch?"

"I'll be happy to do that. I've been starving all morning!" Millie tells Mom.

Millie looks for Jess, but doesn't see her. "Jess!" she calls.

"I'm outside," replies Jess. Jess is Millie's little sis. She's just six.

"How's it going?" asks Millie. "You seem sad."

"I'm fine," sobs Jess.

"You're not fine," Millie tells Jess. "You're crying! What's got my sis down? Please tell me."

"Granny teased me on the phone," Jess frowns. "She told me I look ravishing!"

Millie smiles. It's plain that Jess doesn't understand the meaning of *ravishing*.

"Granny isn't teasing you. In fact, I'd like Granny to say that I'm ravishing," Millie explains.

"You'd like that?" asks Jess. "It wouldn't make you sad?"

"Nope," replies Millie. "In fact, it would be sweet if she told me that."

"But isn't Granny saying that I need to eat?" Jess asks Millie. "That I'm too skinny?"

"I've got good news, Jess," smiles Millie. "Granny doesn't mean that. She's saying you're really good looking!"

"She is?" asks Jess. "She really doesn't mean that I need to eat more?"

"Nope!" Millie replies once more. "But I need to eat more. Let's go help Mom make lunch. I'm starving!"

"Me too!" yells Jess. "I'll race you to the kitchen."

Will Tigers Disappear?

Written by Shane McIntire

Prefixes *un-, re-, mis-, dis-, non-*

disappear	mistreat	unlawfully
unknown	disgrace	reclaim
recycle	reuse	nonprofit
replace	unhappy	

High-Frequency Words

of	have	the	they
are	a	people	to
build	what	there	some
many	only	answer	would
give	live	buy	

133

Most of us have not seen tigers in the wild.
Tigers pad along in forests. They are white and
gold with black stripes. These colors help tigers
blend in so they can hide and hunt for food. Such
big cats need lots of meat. A tiger can eat 50
pounds of meat in a single meal!

Tigers are strong and fast. A tiger can leap 30 feet. Look out deer! A tiger roams for miles and miles looking for food.

A tiger makes a den in a cave, a hollow tree, or heavy brush. Most tigers sleep when it's daylight and hunt at night.

But now tigers are in trouble. Tigers need land with trees for homes. People cut down trees to build houses and to clear land for growing crops. This means that tiger homes will disappear. Then tigers will not find deer to eat. We may not mean to mistreat tigers, but that is what happens. Tigers can't live with people.

Hunters poach, or unlawfully hunt, tigers. There are rules to keep tigers safe. But some people will not follow rules. Each day, tigers die. How many are left is unknown. We think there may be only about 6,000 tigers left in the world. Will tigers die out?

We hope the answer is NO! People must not let tigers die out. It would be a mistake and a disgrace. We must try to save our tigers. How?

We can give tigers safe places to live away from people. We can reclaim some land for wild homes.

How can we slow cutting of trees? We can
save some wild homes for tigers if we cut back on
things we buy. We can change our habits.

1. Use less paper.
2. Recycle and reuse.

We can also tell others that we need to save tigers in trouble. We can join a club or work with nonprofit groups that fight to save our tigers. If all the tigers die, we can't replace them. Let's try to stop an unhappy ending to this tale.

Mr. Sullivan Goes to Work

Prefixes un-, re-, mis-, dis-, non-

misread	disappoint	unhappy
unlike	unable	rechecked
nonstop	misprint	misspelling
reread	discover	redirected
nonworking	mismatched	misunderstood
nonsense	disagree	

High-Frequency Words

again	said	was
want	the	they
would	to	a
from	you	

Mr. Sullivan looked at his clock. 3:30? Did he misread that? He looked again. He had misread it. It said 2:30. That was good. He did not want to disappoint the players. They would be unhappy if he was late. Being late was unlike him.

Mr. Sullivan checked in his closet for his equipment bag. At first, he was unable to see it. But when he rechecked, he found it.

141

Next he ran to his bus stop. He hoped to catch the nonstop bus to the ballpark. The first bus had a sign that said *No stop.* Was that a misprint or a misspelling? Mr. Sullivan quickly reread the sign. It said *Nonstop.*

At the ballpark, Mr. Sullivan tried to enter at an exit. He did not discover that he misread this sign until an usher redirected him. Then Mr. Sullivan tried to take a nonworking elevator up to the locker room. He did not quite see that sign too.

In the locker room, Mr. Sullivan changed into his uniform. He slipped on mismatched socks. One was brown. The other was black.

On the field before the game, a coach used his hand to chase bugs away from his face. Mr. Sullivan misunderstood and waved back at the coach.

The game started and Mr. Sullivan took his spot behind the catcher. Mr. Sullivan yelled, "Play ball!"

The pitcher fired the first pitch. "Strike!" yelled Mr. Sullivan.

The batter exclaimed, "Strike? Ump Sullivan, you cannot see well!"

"Nonsense," replied Mr. Sullivan. "I disagree with you. I can see perfectly!"

Misplaced Buttons

Prefixes *un-, re-, mis-, dis-, non-*

mistaken	discover	uncover
misplaced	discarded	uncommon
replace	unable	dismiss
nonstop	unlike	nonsense

High-Frequency Words

do	you	only	are
a	the	of	have
what	anything	live	would
who			

Do you think that only humans like shiny things such as rings or fancy buttons? If you do, you are mistaken. Animals called packrats like these things too.

A packrat is a real rat that lives in the western United States. You might find packrats in nests in caves or under plants. You might also discover packrat nests in house walls, attics, or basements.

Packrats make nests out of bits of rock, twigs, and plants such as cactus. But if you find packrat nests, you might uncover surprises. Those nests can also be made with bits of glittering little buttons, bright tiny beads, and other shiny things that humans have misplaced or discarded.

Packrats really like these shiny things. It is not uncommon for a packrat to trade a twig or pebble for anything shiny it sees. A packrat will stop, drop what it has, and replace it with that shiny thing. That packrat is unable to stop itself. It likes shiny stuff!

If packrats live around you, you might find signs of packrat trades. Is an old bright button you left on a table missing? Is a little stone there instead? Did a packrat make a trade with you? Don't dismiss that idea!

When packrats live in houses, people hear them at night. Would you like hearing the nonstop patter of little rat feet in the attic? If you enjoy the sound, you are unlike most folks.

Those noisy packrats might be fighting over shiny things. That seems like nonsense, but who knows?

Stuck in the Mud

Written by Cassie Merin

/j/j, g, dge

Jack	Jake	ridge	gentle	edge
stage	bridge	large	suggested	enjoying

/s/s, c

city	school	south	stage	chance	since
slid	cell	decided	raced	pace	soaked
once	silly	faces	voices	saved	

/k/c, k, ck, ch

Jack	Jake	school	track	acting	cubes	cracks
echoed	crossed	creek	rocked	stuck	quickly	truck

High-Frequency Words

lived	the	to	of
would	a	their	one
someone	door	you	are
once	what	sure	they
there	were		

145

Jack and Jake lived on the ridge far above the city lights. Every morning the twins rode the school bus down the gentle slopes to Oak Trail School on the south edge of town.

After school Jack ran with the track team. Jake went to acting club. He liked being on stage. Then Jack and Jake went home on the bus.

On this rain-soaked day, Jack and Jake would get a chance to help out by using their track and acting skills. It had rained since morning. Suddenly, hail the size of ice cubes pelted down. Lightning flashed and loud cracks of thunder echoed around the bus.

That's when it happened! The bus crossed Old
Creek Bridge and then slid. One tire ended up in
a large roadside mud puddle. Mr. Ford rocked
the bus back and forth, but the tire dug deeper
and deeper. It was stuck in mud.

Mr. Ford tried his cell phone, but it did not work in storms. He had no way to phone for help. Jake suggested that someone go for help. "Jack is on the track team. He can run back to school."

Jack agreed. "It's not far. I will get help. The school will send a tow truck."

Mr. Ford decided that might be the best plan. He gave Jack a poncho and told him to be careful.

Jack waved and then raced down the hill. He tried to pace himself so that he would not tire out too quickly.

Jack saw Miss Sealy. He pounded on the door. "Jack, you are soaked. Why are you here?" she asked.

Once she heard Jack's story, she phoned for a tow truck. She phoned moms and dads telling them what had happened. She and Jack got in her car. She was sure kids on the bus would be upset.

When they got there, kids on the bus were not upset. Jake was making silly faces and voices. He was acting out "The Three Little Pigs" by himself. The kids were enjoying his play.

Jack and Jake had saved the day.

Singing

Spellings of /j/, /s/, /k/

cemented	edge	brick
fence	Ginger	nice
voice	stick	garage
range	chorus	practicing
school	choral	concert
music	change	came

High-Frequency Words

the	to	a
said	you	into
was	again	what's
they	who	

Dad cemented an edge on the old brick fence. Ginger helped. She handed bricks to Dad. As Dad worked, he sang. He had a sweet, nice voice. Ginger sang right along with Dad.

After a bit, Dad said, "Ginger, we're finished. I'll stick this stuff in the garage while you get cleaned up.

As Ginger went into her house, Dad sang "Home on the Range." That was the song that Ginger's third-grade chorus was practicing.

"Mom," said Ginger, "Dad is singing a song that my chorus will do in our next school choral concert."

Mom leaned out the window to hear what Dad was singing. Then she smiled. "Let me play an old CD for you, Ginger."

Ginger sat next to Mom as music played. A child's voice on the old CD sang "Home on the Range." When it ended, Ginger said, "That voice is so sweet and nice! Can you play it again?"

Mom did and this time Ginger sang along with it. "You and the third grader on that old CD make a splendid duet," said Mom.

"That's a third grader singing on that old CD? What's her name?" asked Ginger.

"It's not a girl," smiled Mom. "It's a boy."

"A boy!" said Ginger. "It sounds like a girl."

"In third grade, boys' and girls' voices sound alike," explained Mom. "In teen years, boys' voices change. They get much deeper."

"Who is that boy?" Ginger asked. "He sings so well."

Just then, Dad came in. "That's the boy," Mom said.

"Dad!" cried Ginger.

"And he still sings so well," added Mom.

Ring!

Spellings of /j/, /s/, /k/

cell	pick	counter	center
large	garbage	truck	city
traffic	budge	school	choices
chord	cowbells	chickens	clucking
circus	music	celery	sticks
came	concert	chorus	quickly

High-Frequency Words

a	want	to
the	of	was
there	one	could
they	your	

When Mom got a new cell phone, she did not want it to sound like other phones. She wanted to pick just the right ring for hers. So Mom tried a lot of ring tones at a counter in the center of the cell phone store. The clerk at the store helped her.

First Mom tried an odd tone that sounded like horns on a large garbage truck. It made Mom jump up! It made the clerk jump up! "That sound makes me feel like I'm stuck in city traffic that will not budge!" she exclaimed.

The next tone sounded better. It sounded like school bells, but it was still loud. Mom felt there had to be better choices.

The third tone was the sound of a banjo being strummed. The clerk enjoyed this tone. But the sound of a banjo chord did not thrill Mom.

The clerk helped Mom try more choices. Mom tested tones that sounded like cowbells chiming, chickens clucking, dogs barking, and circus music. One tone even sounded like a person crunching celery sticks.

Then Mom found a ring tone choice that came from a recording of a real concert. It was a chorus quickly singing, "Your phone is ringing!" Mom liked that. She enjoyed how the voices blended. Mom had a ring tone that she liked! The clerk put it on Mom's cell phone.

Mom thanked the clerk, shook hands with him, and left the store.

Suddenly, Mom could hear choral voices in her purse. They sang, "Your phone is ringing!"

Mom could not wait to say hello!

Friendly Kindness

Written by Robert Stirim

Suffixes -ly, -ful, -ness, -less, -able, -ible

illness	careful	cheerful
suddenly	sensible	skillful
rapidly	proudly	sadly
kindness	wonderful	finally
dependable		

High-Frequency Words

been	the	a	was
to	you	are	would
want	come	very	one
watch	move	your	who

It had not been the best week for Travis.
He had been stuck in bed for six days with a sore
throat. Now it was time to try out for the soccer
team, but Travis was weak from his illness, and
his dad wouldn't let him play.

Travis went outside and kicked and stamped
his feet.

"Be careful. You might land on the ground!"
Travis spun around. A boy in a wheelchair was
sitting in the next yard. He gave Travis a cheerful
smile.

"Why are you so upset?" the boy asked.

Travis was startled. He looked at the boy and
scowled. He explained his problem.

Suddenly Travis felt bad. He wasn't being sensible. The boy in the chair would never be able to play soccer.

"My name's Travis," he said.

"I'm Mike," the boy replied. "Want to play chess?"

Travis stopped. Chess was for brains. "Come on, I'll teach you," said Mike.

That's how Travis started playing chess. Each
day he and Mike played outside in Mike's yard.

Mike was very skillful at chess and beat Travis
every time. But Travis rapidly got better and
made Mike play hard.

"I must be a brain," Travis admitted one day.
"I really like this game."

Other kids stopped to watch Travis and Mike play. Mike had five chess sets, so his mom set up more tables.

"Come and play," she told them.

"Now I've got a chess team," Mike boasted proudly.

Travis smiled. "This is not the team I expected to be on," he thought.

Each day that summer, the chess club met in Mike's yard.

Then one day Mike told Travis that he had to move to Boston to be near his new doctor.

"He'll help me get well," Mike said. "Keep on playing chess."

"I will," Travis replied sadly.

The day Mike left, his mom went to Travis.

"Thanks for your kindness to Mike," she said. "He had a wonderful summer."

Travis was silent. Finally he spoke.

"That's not the way I see it," he said. "It was Mike who was dependable and showed kindness to me."

On TV

Suffixes –ly, -ful, -ness, -less, -able, -iible

eagerly	weekly	remarkable	sensible
wasteful	useful	playful	graceful
dependable	sweetness	kindness	simply
quickly	spotless	reckless	breakable
handfuls	endless	helpless	tasteless
really	badly	loudly	truthful
hopeful			

High-Frequency Words

the	people	to	their
of	do	whole	into
are	though	work	they
one			

In homes all over the United States, people eagerly tune in to see Mac, the TV cook. On his weekly TV program, Mac makes remarkable meals. People then cook those same meals at home in their own kitchens.

Mac's TV program shows sensible ways to make splendid breakfasts, lunches, and suppers.

165

Mac is never wasteful. He has loads of useful cooking tips.

Plus, Mac makes it look so easy! On TV, Mac is playful, graceful, dependable, and clever. He is filled with sweetness and shows kindness to his TV helpers. Mac makes his meals simply and quickly in his spotless TV kitchen.

Yet TV cameras do not show the whole story about Mac. When his fans do not see him, Mac is not graceful in the kitchen. He is reckless. He slams into things and spills pots and pans all over the place! He breaks most things that are breakable. He wastes handfuls of food with each meal he makes. Mac needs an endless amount of aprons to look clean and neat on TV.

Even worse, without his kitchen helpers around, Mac is helpless. The meals he makes by himself are tasteless. Mac really needs people to tell him how to cook.

And even though Mac needs his helpers, he treats them badly. He yells at them loudly and is not always truthful with them.

Still Mac's helpers work hard, but not because of Mac. They are hopeful that they can help people in the United States make better meals. They are also hopeful that one day, Mac will quit his TV show and let them really do the cooking!

Helpful Julia

Suffixes –ly, -ful, -ness, -less, -able, -ible

helpful	useful	quickly	sadly
playful	tightly	spotless	eagerly
helpless	sortable	sensible	loudly
kindness	huggable		

High-Frequency Words

was	wanted	to
do	the	said
a	you	into
work	money	are

Sara's little sister Julia was just three years old. But she still wanted to be helpful. She wanted to do useful things around her house.

When Julia woke up, she quickly rushed to the kitchen. She wanted to help make breakfast. But the table was set and breakfast was already made. Julia ate hers, but sadly said, "I want to be helpful."

Mom gave Julia a playful hug. Julia hugged Mom back tightly.

After breakfast, Julia tried to help make the house spotless. Dad swept the kitchen, and Julia eagerly tried to pick things up. But Julia kept getting in the way. Dad bent down next to Julia and gave her a hug. "Julia, you can help me by sitting by the table for a moment."

Julia gave Dad a tight hug back and sat by the table. Julia felt helpless.

Later, Sara was sorting dirty laundry. Laundry was sortable into three piles: whites, darks, and lights. Julia tried to help, but she mixed up lights and whites. Sara gave Julia a hug and said, "Julia, it is more sensible for me to do it!"

Julia gave Sara a tight hug back and sadly looked for different work to do. Then Julia saw Mom sitting at the table. Mom read the mail and said loudly, "Bills! Bills! Bills! I wish we did not owe so much money!"

Julia reached up to Mom. Mom put Julia on her lap. Julia hugged Mom tightly and said, "Do not be sad, Mom."

Mom smiled and hugged Julia back. "You are filled with kindness and so huggable, Julia," she said.

"And helpful?" asked Julia.

"And helpful!" said Mom.

Camping and Climbing

Written by Charis Baronne

Silent consonants

whistled	listen	designed	know	signs	climbing
wrist	gnats	limb	wriggled	crumb	rustling
combed	wren	knee-deep	wrestled	wrung	

High-Frequency Words

would	your	said
were	what	to
where	again	a
the	into	have
was	you	done

Stan whistled so that we would listen. "This path is designed to test your skills," Stan said. Ben, Liz, and Rick were on my team.

"We will use what we know about hiking and camping," Ben said. "We must read signs and check our maps to know where to go."

When Stan whistled again, we were off! We started by climbing up a huge hill. Liz slipped on rocks, but I grabbed her wrist and helped her up. At the top, we found the path. We went into the forest together.

Gnats buzzed around our heads. We waved our hands and brushed them away. Soon, we came to a place where a big tree limb had crashed to the ground.

"That must have happened when the storm came," Rick noted. We wriggled under that limb.

Our tired team stopped to eat lunch in silence. When we had finished, not a single crumb was left!

"It is hot and dry," Liz pointed out. "We must drink plenty of liquid."

"Listen!" I said quickly. "Can you hear that rustling sound?"

We combed the grass. We found a wren in her nest, with fuzzy chicks nestled under her wings. We went happily back to our trail without bothering those sleepy wrens.

Our next task was to cross the bog on an old rope bridge. But when Ben stepped on that bridge, it broke! Splash! He fell into the muddy bog. When he got up, he was knee-deep in brown muck. He trudged slowly across the bog as Rick, Liz, and I crossed on stepping stones.

Ben wrestled off his shoes and wrung out his socks. Then he got up and we set off. As we came around a bend, we saw our camp! We ran quickly to reach Stan. He patted us on our backs.

"That is a job well done!" he said proudly. Even Ben with his wet socks grinned at that.

Barb's Robot

Consonant Patterns *wr, kn, gn, st, mb*

design	wrists	thumbs	knuckles
knees	climb	wrinkles	write
sign	whistle	comb	toothbrush
knobs	gnats	listened	

High-Frequency Words

to	a	do
what	said	you
want	could	have
work	off	

"I am going to design a robot. It will do what I tell it," said Barb. "I will design it on my easel."

"It will do what you tell it?" asked Sal.

"Yes," said Barb. "But stay back. I do not want to show you my design until I'm finished."

On her easel, Barb drew a robot design. Her robot looked human. It had arms, wrists, and hands. It even had fingers and thumbs with knuckles. It had knees so it could bend its legs and climb. It even had cute little wrinkles next to its smiling mouth.

"If I have designed this robot well, it will do a lot that humans can do," Barb told Sal. "It will write and sign its name. It will whistle. It will get things for me. It will even use a comb and toothbrush."

"Do you have to turn knobs to make it work?" asked Sal.

"No, I just tell it what to do," explained Barb.

Just then a few gnats buzzed by Barb and Sal. "Yikes!" said Barb. "Chase those gnats away!"

Sal listened, waved her hand, and the gnats buzzed off fast. Then Sal asked, "Can I see the robot design?"

Barb showed Sal the design. "It looks just like me!" cried Sal.

After Sal studied the design more, she asked, "How can you test to see if this robot will do what you tell it?"

"I just did test it," said Barb. "I had it chase away gnats."

Sal looked surprised, but then she got it.

"But I can't whistle," said Sal with a grin.

Game Day

Consonant Patterns *wr, kn, gn, st, mb*

Gnarled	climb	well-known	wrote
sign	climbers	thumbs	fasten
knots	knuckles	wrists	knit
write	design	signs	lambs
whistled	wrinkled	Knight	numb

High-Frequency Words

the	was	to	they
of	a	two	they
their	from	could	do
watched	there	were	some

The last day at Camp Gnarled Tree was game day. Ranger Norm had to judge camp kids as they did camp tests.

For the first test, kids had to climb the well-known gnarled tree. This twisted tree sat in the middle of camp. When a kid made it to the top, Ranger Norm wrote the kid's name on a sheet of paper. Next to each name, Ranger Norm had to sign his own name.

179

Eleven kids made it to the top! Ranger Norm gave climbers two thumbs up as they did it. Then he wrote their names and his name on the paper.

Next, kids had to skip from the first stone to the last. The stones went around the camp's west side. Ranger Norm knew that all the kids could do that, so he wrote the names of all fifty camp kids on his paper. He signed his name after each one.

After skipping, kids had to fasten tricky knots. Ranger Norm got dizzy as he watched fingers, knuckles, and wrists knit knots fast! He got even dizzier as he had to write more names and sign his name over and over.

There were more tests. Some were odd! Kids had to design camp signs. They made the sounds of cows, horses, and lambs. They whistled bird songs. They wrinkled their noses and smelled different flowers.

For each test, Ranger Norm had to write more names and sign his name over and over and over!

The kids did well. They each got a medal that read *Knight of the Gnarled Tree*. When the day was finished at last, Ranger Norm was happy. And his writing hand was numb!